PAUL POGBA

MAKING HIS MARK ON THE SOCCER WORLD

BRIAN TRUSDELL

First Edition
First Printing, 2019

Book design by Jake Slavik
Cover design by Jake Slavik
Photographs ©: Christian Liewig/Abaca/Sipa USA/AP Images, cover (foreground), cover (right), 88; Jean Catuffe/Getty Images Sport/Getty Images Europe/Getty Images, 4; Dean Mouhtaropoulos/Getty Images Sport/Getty Images Europe/Getty Images, 6; Peter Dejong/AP Images, 8, 12; Ekaterina Pokrovsky/Shutterstock Images, 14; pavalena/Shutterstock Images, 17; smolaw/Shutterstock Images, 20; Yuryev Pavel/Shutterstock Images, 24; PhotoLondonUK/Shutterstock Images, 29; Matthew Peters/Manchester United/Getty Images, 30, 33; Andrew Matthews/URN:10006652/Press Association/AP Images, 35; Dave Thompson/PA Wire URN:13959241/Press Association/AP Images, 39; Luca Bruno/AP Images, 40; Massimo Pinca/AP Images, 45, 49; Gero Breloer/AP Images, 47; Efrem Lukatsky/AP Images, 50; Dave Winter/Icon Sport/Cal Sport Media/AP Images, 55; Kirsty Wigglesworth/AP Images, 57; Matteo Bottanelli/Sipa/AP Images, 58, 64; Matteo Ciambelli/1411231131/Sipa/AP Images, 61; Philip Oldham/Sportimage/Cal Sport Media/AP Images, 67; Martin Meissner/AP Images, 68, 72; John Spencer/Sipa/AP Images, 75; KCS Presse/Splash News/Newscom, 76; Jon Super/AP Images, 80; Anders Wiklund/TT News Agency/AP Images, 83; Matt Dunham/AP Images, 87; Hassan Ammar/AP Images, 90; Elmar Kremser/Sven Simon/picture-alliance/dpa/AP Images, 94; Matthias Schrader/AP Images, 98; Kyodo/AP Images, 101

Design Elements ©: Shutterstock

Press Box Books, an imprint of Press Room Editions.

Library of Congress Control Number: 2018952199

ISBN:
978-1-63494-049-8 (paperback)
978-1-63494-061-0 (epub)
978-1-63494-073-3 (hosted ebook)

Distributed by North Star Editions, Inc.
2297 Waters Drive
Mendota Heights, MN 55120
www.northstareditions.com
Printed in the United States of America

TABLE OF CONTENTS

Paul Pogba brings the ball upfield for France during the team's World Cup qualifying game against the Netherlands in Amsterdam.

CHAPTER 1
POGBOOM!

More than 50,000 fans, most of them dressed in orange, filled the stands at the Amsterdam Arena, loudly cheering the Netherlands national soccer team. Some waved flags and banners. Many hurled insults at the opposing French national team. But in an instant, they all went silent.

French defender Laurent Koscielny intercepted a pass near the midfield line. He quickly sent it to teammate Dimitri Payet on the left. Then Payet squared the ball into the middle of the field. His unmarked teammate, Paul Pogba, received it.

Pogba, a central midfielder, took one touch forward. The Dutch captain, Kevin Strootman, gave Pogba space. Positioned 35 yards from the goal, Pogba sensed his opportunity. So the Frenchman wound up and unleashed a rocket of a shot. The ball knuckled, swerved, and dipped to the left. Dutch goalie Maarten

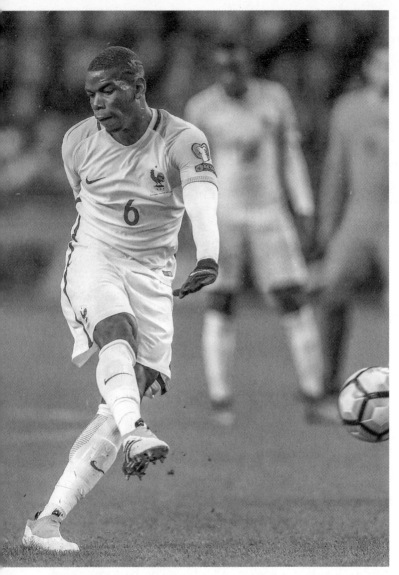

Pogba blasts a shot into the goal to give France a
lead over the Netherlands.

Stekelenburg dived. He was able to get his hands to the ball, but that was not enough. The ball glanced off his fingers and deflected into the net.

"Great goal!" screamed the television announcer.

Pogba simply nodded his head as his French teammates mobbed him.

Powerful shots were nothing new for Pogba. Although he was only 23 years old at the time, he had established himself on two of the biggest club teams in Europe. His physical presence, vision, and technical ability on the ball made him a force in the central midfield. And when the opportunity arose, Pogba had proven he could score goals, too.

This wasn't any ordinary goal, though. The game was on October 10, 2016. France was in Amsterdam, the Netherlands, for a challenging road game in FIFA World Cup qualifying. Only one team from the qualifying group would automatically advance to the 2018 World Cup in Russia. Pogba's score put France up 1–0 against one of its biggest rivals. The Netherlands had finished third at the 2014 World Cup. It had not lost a World Cup qualifying game since 2001, a stretch of 33 games. But thanks to Pogba's goal, that streak ended.

Teammates celebrate with Pogba after his goal against the Netherlands.

France went on to win 1–0. Now with momentum, the team known as Les Bleus went on to win five of the final seven games to finish first in the qualifying group. That secured an automatic berth to the World Cup, despite playing in one of the most difficult groups in Europe.

Though one of the younger players on the team, Pogba played a major role. He started and played the entire 90 minutes in the seven of 10 matches for which he was healthy. And in one of France's other biggest

FRENCH NATIONAL TEAM

The French national team debuted in 1904. Since winning its first World Cup in 1998, France has established itself as a power in the sport. The team, known as Les Bleus for its signature blue jerseys, plays most home games at Stade de France in a Paris suburb. During the 1980s, midfielder Michel Platini became France's first big star. Midfielder Zinedine Zidane led the team to its greatest successes, including the 1998 World Cup. Other stars have included Just Fontaine, Thierry Henry, Lilian Thuram, and Patrick Vieira.

games, against Sweden, he scored again. This time he used his big body to hold off his defender in the box. When a free kick came his way, Pogba used his head to redirect it into the net.

These types of plays had come to be expected of Pogba. He had been playing at the top level of European club soccer since 2011, when he was a teenager. Three years later, at age 21, he had been named the top young player at the 2014 World Cup. And at age 25, he was still considered a young player going into the 2018 tournament.

Tall, fast, and strong, Pogba has a clear physical advantage over most opponents. But he also possesses unique technical skills: dribbling, passing, heading, and, when the opportunity arises, shooting. Altogether, he is one of the world's best midfielders from one penalty box to the other. That's why Manchester United had paid a record transfer fee to obtain him in the summer of 2016. The popular English club spent €105 million ($116 million) to recruit the young star from Juventus of Italy.

Pogba is also a star for who he is as a person. Dynamic and charismatic on the field, he carries those qualities to all he does.

Pogba is famous for his "dab" goal celebrations and changing hairstyles. A December 2017 news report said Pogba had featured 20 hairstyles in the 18 months prior. Throughout his career, he's had everything from fades to Mohawks to shaved-in designs, with any color one could imagine. He often introduces a new style for big games.

But his interests extend beyond what he does on the soccer field. Fluent in four languages—English, French, Italian, and Spanish—Pogba is also interested in fashion, music, and culture.

Fans experience his personality and varied interests through his active social media accounts. More than 24 million users follow him on Instagram, with 5 million more on Twitter. They see frequent pictures and videos of Pogba showing off his dance moves, new hairstyles, and adventures with friends.

As popular as Pogba is around the world, however, his style also invites critics. Especially after his record transfer to Manchester United, scrutiny from fans and media increased. They accused him of being distracted. Prior to the 2018 World Cup, Denmark's coach asked, "Does he only think about his haircuts?" These types of accusations frustrate Pogba.

As his goal against the Netherlands showed, Pogba had great potential going into the 2018 World Cup.

"I am less entitled to make mistakes than others," Pogba said. "I went from the biggest transfer in the world to the most criticized player in the world."

"I am less entitled to make mistakes than others. I went from the biggest transfer in the world to the most criticized player in the world."

– PAUL POGBA

That doesn't mean he is planning to change, though. Pogba makes no apologies for being a showman—both on and off the field.

"I'm having fun," he said, "and that's the only answer I can give to all those people who criticize me or who think I am this or that."

But after a mediocre 2017–18 season with Manchester United, the pressure was starting to build. Did he really have what it took to live up to his status as the most expensive player in soccer?

At age 25, Pogba was just entering the prime of his career. And now that he had helped France qualify for the World Cup, he had the perfect opportunity to prove his doubters wrong on the biggest stage in the world of sports.

Paul grew up approximately 20 miles east of central Paris, where the Eiffel Tower is located.

CHAPTER 2
FROM THE STREETS OF PARIS

Born on March 15, 1993, Paul Labile Pogba grew up in a poor area of France, immediately outside Paris. He lived in a tall white apartment building in the suburb of Roissy-en-Brie. It was a public housing complex, meaning the government helped pay for it. Most of the people who lived there were immigrants from African countries such as Guinea, Mali, and Senegal.

Those countries had once been French colonies, and many people who lived there moved to France to escape poverty at home. That was the case for Paul's family. His parents were from Guinea, a small country in West

Africa. Although France offered more opportunities than Guinea, life was still hard. The apartment Paul grew up in was small. He shared it with his mother, two older twin brothers, and two girl cousins.

Still, life in the cramped apartment was a far cry from Guinea. Paul's father, Fassou Antoine Pogba Hebelamou, was from a town call Pela, Guinea. It's a bush village on the edge of the rainforest. Accessible only by 4x4 truck, Pela is 90 miles from the nearest city. But for eight months of the year, floods cut off Pela from the rest of the world.

It's from this village that the Pogba family inherits its name. Paul's grandfather's name was Hebelamou, but people called him "Pogba." In the tribal language of Guerze, it means "reverential son," someone who is respected by his family. Paul's grandfather adopted the name and gave it to his son, Fassou.

Fassou first moved to Paris in the mid-1960s. He found jobs working in telecommunications and then as a teacher. While not working, Fassou played soccer and remained a loyal fan of the Guinean national team, known as the Syli. But he was lonely. In the late 1980s, when he was 50, Fassou returned to Guinea to look for a wife. He arrived in the capital of Conakry, Guinea,

Guinea gained independence from France in 1958.

where he lived with his younger brother and one of his sisters.

It was there he met Yeo Moriba, a woman in her 20s. Besides their age, the two had other differences. Fassou was Christian, and Moriba was Muslim. Fassou was working class, and Moriba was from a prominent family. Her great uncle had been the prime minister of Guinea. He also briefly served as the country's interim president. Despite their differences, Fassou and Moriba shared a passion for soccer. Her cousin even played briefly for a successful pro team in Conakry.

The two married, and Moriba soon gave birth to twin boys: Florentin and Mathias. The family lived in Conakry for two years before permanently leaving the country for France in the early 1990s. The Pogbas settled in Roissy-en-Brie. Within a year they had another son, Paul.

But the family would not remain together. Two years after Paul was born, his parents separated. His father remained in the apartment, whereas his mother moved to the housing estate a few miles away with the three boys. She also took in her sister's two girls, Marie-Yvette and Poupette.

Paul's mother worked several jobs to meet the family's financial needs. She was a maid in a hotel, a supermarket cashier, and an aide for people with disabilities. Although Paul's dad was separated from his wife, he remained active in his sons' lives. He attended their soccer games and took them to watch Paris Saint-Germain, a popular team in France's top division, Ligue 1.

Even from a young age, Paul was an active kid. He liked to turn on music and dance, and he loved playing outside. He especially loved to play soccer.

Paul began playing soccer when he was four. Though his brothers were more than two years older than him, he followed them around everywhere, including to the soccer field. At first, they said he was too young to play with them and their friends. But soon Paul proved that he more than belonged on the field with the older kids.

The neighborhood kids spent many hours outside playing pickup games at City Stade. The local field was approximately the size of a basketball court. It was only big enough for five-on-five games. But it was the perfect place for Paul to spend his days and improve his skills.

"He was always curious to know things, even as a small child. He always wanted to learn new things," Paul's dad said. "We always encouraged him to do lots of things and to follow his interests. When I saw him play football for the first time, though, I could see that his technique was very good."

Even though Paul was younger, Florentin and Mathias showed him no slack. If Paul was knocked

Paul and his brothers developed a love for the game while playing on a small field near their home.

down and looked ready to tear up, they told him to stop crying and get up. Before long, though, Paul had more than proven that he belonged.

In time, the Pogba boys graduated from street games to the local soccer club, Union Sportive de Roissy-en-Brie, or US Roissy. The team was based at a location that was a five-minute walk from their apartment. And as with the five-a-side games, Florentin and Mathias joined first, followed by Paul in September 1999.

Paul was only six years old at the time. The club's stadium was nothing more than a dirt field with some seats. But this wasn't five-a-side pickup soccer. This was 11-on-11. Real soccer.

The coach, Aziz Keftouna, had worked with Paul's brothers, so he knew how competitive the family was. But Keftouna was amazed by Paul's maturity. Instead of trying to score goals, Paul was looking to pass the ball. Keftouna challenged him to juggle the ball 150 times: 50 on his right foot, 50 on his left, and 50 with his head. Three days later, Paul returned. With the team counting, he showed his coach he could do it.

The US Roissy coaches were impressed not only with Paul's skills but also with his desire to learn and improve. He hated to lose, though with Paul the team didn't lose often. And by the time he turned 10, scouts from bigger clubs were coming to watch him play.

US ROISSY

US Roissy is a local recreation and sports club in the Paris suburb of Roissy-en-Brie, where Paul grew up. The club offers programs in several sports, the most popular being soccer. The soccer program began in the 1950s. Its teams play in the Seine-et-Marne leagues and occasionally against regional competition. The club's colors are red and blue.

Two years later, Fassou believed Paul had outgrown US Roissy. Le Havre, a team in France's second division, had expressed interest in Paul. But he was only 12, and Le Havre was three hours away on the northern coast of France. Paul's mom thought he was too young to move away.

Even so, Paul needed to find a higher level of play. So US Roissy's Under-13 coach, Bijou Tati, contacted the manager of US Torcy, the best youth team in the area. That club had produced players who went on to professional clubs in France, England, and Italy. And even better, US Torcy was only 20 minutes away from Paul's home.

US Torcy manager Stephane Albe agreed to take a look at Paul, and the coach came away impressed. After watching him in a game, Albe offered Paul a spot on the team. Because the club wasn't far away, Paul could play at US Torcy while living at home.

The new club proved to be a good fit for Paul. Though US Torcy played at a higher level than US Roissy, Paul continued to thrive. Within months he was US Torcy's best player and was named the team's captain.

Paul was a complete package: physically big, strong, and fast with a great set of skills, soccer knowledge, and desire. So it was little surprise that he started to attract attention from even bigger clubs. Le Havre scouts continued to monitor Paul. So did scouts from some Ligue 1 teams.

A year after joining US Torcy, Paul was already prepared to move on. Though Paul was still only 13, Le Havre was able to convince his mother to let him try out for its Under-14 team in November 2006. Paul performed so well that the club spoke to his parents. Team officials presented a plan for Paul that included both education and soccer training. This time, his parents agreed to let him go.

It was time for Paul to take another big leap.

US TORCY

Union Sportive de Torcy, or US Torcy, is an amateur sports club. Founded in 1942, it is based in the town of Torcy, France. The club originally offered programs in soccer, gymnastics, and bowling. It has teams for players from ages 6 to 66.

Le Havre is a port city in France's Normandy region northwest of Paris.

CHAPTER 3
OPPORTUNITIES ARISE

The move to Le Havre was a big step for Paul. He was living 150 miles from home, away from the rest of his family. And this wasn't simply recreational soccer. Paul was now part of an academy for a professional club.

Le Havre had played mostly in France's second division. But being a professional club, it was able to pay for Paul's education. It also paid for his housing and training. By selecting Paul for the academy, Le Havre showed that it believed Paul might someday become a full professional. And very early on, it was clear that Paul's professional career might take him to clubs much bigger than Le Havre.

"My first memory of him was his personality," Le Havre's chief scout Franck Sale said, in an interview translated from French. "He had excellent technique and ability, and (he) was already powerful and strong. But it was his personality—he had lots of confidence."

This confidence helped Paul in his transition to the academy team. Growing up, he was used to always being the best player on the field. With Le Havre, his teammates all had the same background. Once again, though, Paul soon showed that he had the ability to be the best on this team, too. But knowing his personality, club officials made a point of being strict with him.

LE HAVRE AC

Based in the port city of Le Havre, Le Havre Athletic Club has spent most of its history in France's second division, or Ligue 2. Founded in 1872 as a track and rugby club, Le Havre added soccer in 1894. The club is known for its youth development. In addition to Pogba, Le Havre has produced stars including Ibrahim Ba, Lassana Diarra, Benjamin Mendy, and Dmitri Payet.

"Paul came from an amateur club and, without knocking them, there were things that had to be put in place," said Mickael Le Baillif, Paul's first coach at Le Havre. "He was still playing a very pure and natural form of football. He had a tendency not to follow instructions. During his first season, we also had to teach him to get more of a handle on his emotions."

Paul progressed quickly. Arriving as a 14-year-old, he began on Le Havre's U-15 team. The league included youth teams from major first-division powers, such as Paris Saint-Germain. With Paul playing a leading role, Le Havre finished second in that 2007–08 season.

He gained further attention in the 2008 U-15 Coupe Nationale, a tournament played among regional teams. With pro scouts looking on, Paul took a leading role for the team from Normandy, France, where Le Havre is located. He was also chosen as team captain. Though Normandy fell short of the championship, Paul made a strong impression. He was already much bigger, faster, and stronger than players his same age. Scouts also praised his technical ability and vision.

The next step for Paul was a call up to France's U-16 national team. Paul had his first opportunity in September 2008, when he played in a friendly game.

That led to an opportunity to play in the Val-de-Marne tournament a month later. Coach Guy Ferrier thought Paul played well, but he believed the midfielder could be much better.

"He certainly worked hard, but he always went too far," Ferrier said after one game. "He thought he could manage everything himself."

Scouts watching the tournament focused on Paul's upside. David Friio, a scout from Manchester United, was particularly impressed. After watching Paul in one game, he immediately called his bosses. The English club dispatched three more officials to watch Paul in the final two games of the tournament.

Back at Le Havre in 2008–09, the club moved up to a new age division. The competition got tougher, too. But the coaches believed in Paul. They made him a central midfielder, tasking him with running the offense. He was also made team captain.

Le Havre again finished second. And Friio continued to follow Paul, traveling all over France to watch him play. He was constantly pushing his bosses to take a closer look at the talented young player.

In March 2009, just before Paul's 16th birthday, an opportunity arose. Friio arranged for Paul and his

Nicknamed "The Theatre of Dreams," Manchester United's Old Trafford is one of soccer's most famous stadiums.

parents to fly to Manchester, England. It was a big trip. Paul walked around the famous Old Trafford stadium. He met United superstar Cristiano Ronaldo. The team also gave Paul's dad a red Manchester United tie. He immediately put it on and didn't take it off. Most important, though, Paul and his parents met with United's iconic manager Alex Ferguson.

As Paul sat in Ferguson's office, listening to the manager explain how the club was not shy about playing talented players regardless of their age, Paul made up his mind. He wanted to play for Manchester United.

**Paul's future looked bright when he joined
Manchester United as a 16-year-old in 2009.**

CHAPTER 4
RISING WITH THE RED DEVILS

Most of Paul's teammates and coaches were on vacation when the news broke that he had agreed to join Manchester United's youth academy. It was July 30, 2009—Paul was only four months past his 16th birthday.

Le Havre officials were furious. Paul had signed an agreement that said he would remain with the team. The club accused Manchester United of bribing Paul's parents so he would break that deal. The president of Le Havre, Jean-Pierre Louvel, claimed Manchester United had paid Paul's parents €100,000 ($140,000) each and bought his mother a house. United called the claims "complete nonsense." Still, Louvel said he was "deeply disappointed" about the matter.

US Torcy officials could only smirk at the situation. The team put out a sarcastic press release suggesting Le Havre had acted the same when it signed Paul away from them.

At the heart of the issue was the question of payment. In professional soccer, teams usually purchase the rights to a player, rather than swapping players in a trade. Many teams, such as Le Havre, take players into their academies with the hope that they will someday move on to the pro level. They invest money in those players. If one becomes a star, the club can sell him on to a bigger team for a big profit. Le Havre accused Manchester United of skirting those rules by recruiting Paul to join its academy rather than buying his rights.

Le Havre appealed to FIFA, soccer's world governing body. The French Football Federation supported Le Havre. It delayed the official transfer and refused to call Paul into the U-17 national team for six months.

When FIFA finally ruled, though, it sided in favor of Manchester United. The agreement Paul had signed had said no other French teams could recruit him. Because Manchester United is in England, FIFA said

Paul plays for Manchester United's youth team in a 2009 game against Birmingham City.

the agreement didn't apply to them. Finally, in June 2010, Manchester United and Le Havre agreed on terms, and Paul's transfer became official.

By then Paul had already been in Manchester for nine months. He began with the club's academy team and moved in with a host family, the Dalbys. They lived near the team's training center in Carrington, England. The Dalbys were also hosting Davide Petrucci, an academy player from Italy. He and Paul became friends, and Davide even taught Paul a little Italian. This would help Paul later, but for now he had another problem: he didn't speak much English. This made it hard for him to understand what his coaches and teammates were saying.

Paul made up for that with his talent and size. Already, he was much taller than the other kids on the academy team. Plus, he had incredible skill on the ball and surprising coordination for someone of his height. As had been the case when he was younger, Paul also impressed the coaches with his desire to win. He was often the last to leave after training, always practicing juggling, free kicks, and penalties.

Paul started his second season with the academy team. By November 2010, though, he received word that he had been promoted to the reserve team. This was a big change, especially for a 17-year-old. He would now be playing with full professionals. His opponents would be other talented players battling for Premier League roster spots.

Paul battles with a Portsmouth player during the 2011 FA Youth Cup, which Manchester United went on to win.

After splitting his time between the reserves and the academy in 2010–11, Paul was assigned permanently to the reserves for his second season.

Manager Alex Ferguson added that Paul would soon have a shot with the first team.

"I mean if we hold Pogba back, what's going to happen? He's going to leave," Ferguson told reporters. "You know, in a couple of years' time when his contract is going to finish. So we have to give him the opportunity to see how he can do in the first team, and he's got great ability."

Paul made his first team debut on September 20, 2011. He entered a League Cup match as a second-half substitute. The League Cup is the second-tier tournament in England. It's often a place where top teams let their young players gain experience. Four months later, a better opportunity arose. Paul made his Premier League debut on January 31, 2012. Again, he entered the game as a second-half substitute. The season included one more debut that spring. Paul entered as a substitute in a Europa League game against Athletic Bilbao of Spain. That is the second-tier European continental tournament. In all, Paul played in seven

"I mean if we hold Pogba back, what's going to happen? He's going to leave."

– ALEX FERGUSON
FORMER MANCHESTER
UNITED MANAGER

games with the first team during the 2011–12 season, all as a substitute.

Still only 18 years old, Paul was seen as one of the brightest young stars in England. But his team was filled with star players, many of them older and more experienced. This made it hard for Paul to find

MANCHESTER UNITED FC

Located in northwest England, Manchester United Football Club is one of the world's most popular sports teams. In 2017, *Forbes* estimated the team was worth $3.7 billion, making it the world's third most valuable team in any sport. Founded in 1878 as the Newton Heath LYR Football Club, the team changed its name to Manchester United in 1902. The team, also known as Man United or the Red Devils, is also one of the most successful in the world. No English team has won as many top-division league titles. In 1968, United also became the first English team to win the European Cup (now Champions League). It won its third European championship in 2008. Manchester United plays at the iconic stadium known as Old Trafford.

playing time. The situation frustrated him, because he believed he was ready for a more important role.

Paul's dissatisfaction came to a head on December 31, 2011, when the last-place Blackburn Rovers came to play at Manchester United. Red Devils midfielder Darren Fletcher was injured. Paul thought he would be allowed to start in Fletcher's place. Instead, Paul sat on the bench the entire game.

He was furious. To make matters worse, Blackburn upset Manchester United 3–2. And then there was word that veteran midfielder Paul Scholes, who had retired only six months earlier, was returning to play. Paul thought he might never get to the first team.

"You're at United, but you're not playing," his brother Mathias said to him. "Perhaps you'd be better off looking for a chance somewhere else."

The good news for Paul was the other teams were interested in him—and those teams were promising he would play.

Despite high expectations, Paul struggled to find a regular role with Manchester United's first team.

Pogba's arrival at Juventus in Italy brought new life to his young career.

CHAPTER 5
GOLDEN BOY

After three seasons with Manchester United, Pogba's contract was about to expire. During the summer of 2012, Manchester United wanted him to sign an extension. Pogba wasn't sure whether he wanted to sign.

Pogba and his family spoke to Oualid Tanazefti, an agent whom he had met when he was 13. Tanazefti brought in another agent, one who had represented some of the game's biggest stars. The agents told Pogba that some of Europe's biggest teams were interested in him. Based on this, they believed he should be paid as a first-team player. Manager Alex Ferguson disagreed. He said Pogba wasn't a regular first-team player yet.

Pogba was conflicted. Manchester United had given him an opportunity, and he wanted to succeed there. But with more playing time elsewhere, he might have a better opportunity if he left.

Ferguson sent defender Patrice Evra to try to convince Pogba to stay. Evra, who is also French, even visited Pogba at his home with his mother and brothers. But Pogba wasn't convinced. He decided not to sign—and the decision had consequences. His mother said Ferguson retaliated by not playing Pogba the rest of the season. Pogba cried in Ferguson's office. Finally, on July 3, it was over.

JUVENTUS FC

Based in Torino, Italy, Juventus Football Club is the country's most popular soccer team, with more than 300 million fans worldwide. It's also Italy's most decorated team, having won more championships than any other club in the Italian league, Coppa Italia, and Italian Super Cup. Juventus has also supplied more players to the Italian national team than any other club. Founded in 1897, Juventus has been famous for its distinctive black-and-white, vertical-striped jerseys since 1903. Sometimes called "The Old Lady," the club has been managed by the Agnelli family since 1923.

Juventus, the most successful team in Italy, signed Pogba to a four-year contract. By the end of the month, Pogba was with his new team in Torino, Italy.

As with Manchester United, Pogba joined a talented team in Juventus. Among his new teammates were legends of the game, including midfielder Andrea Pirlo and goalie Gianluigi Buffon. Unlike in Manchester, though, the team offered an opportunity for Pogba to join those players as a regular player.

It took four games for Pogba to play his first competitive match for Juventus. But he started against Chievo on September 22 and played the full 90 minutes. Two weeks later, he debuted in the Champions League, the annual tournament among Europe's best teams. In this game, Pogba entered as a late substitute against Shakhtar Donetsk of Ukraine. Less than three weeks after that, he scored his first goal for Juventus, an 82nd-minute tally in a 2–0 win over Napoli. The win put Juventus in first place.

The good times continued days later when he scored another big goal, this time heading in the winner in injury time to lead a 2–1 victory over Bologna. *La Repubblica* newspaper called him a "hurricane." Pogba was receiving his opportunity from Juventus manager Antonio Conte, and he wasn't going to waste it.

As he thrived on the field, Pogba found comfort in his new home, too. Italy wasn't completely foreign to him, because his former housemate Davide Petrucci was from Rome, Italy. And unlike in England, where Pogba lived with a host family, he was now old enough to have his own apartment.

Pogba also liked his new teammates, and especially his new manager. Conte saw him as more focused than Ferguson had. Conte also gave the young player more freedom to join the attack. This led to Pogba getting more regular appearances and more starts. And the more Pogba played, the higher the expectations became.

By January 2013, Pogba had his first multiple-goal game, scoring twice in a 4–0 victory over Udinese. With a bleach-blond Mohawk haircut, Pogba was quickly becoming a fan favorite and worldwide sensation. He also became known as Pogboom, because long-range shots were his trademark. By the end of the season, he had scored five goals and helped Juventus to the Serie A title. The team also reached the Champions League quarterfinals that season.

Pogba shoots and scores against Udinese in January 2013.

Pogba's success led to more opportunity. On March 22, only one week after his 20th birthday, he debuted for France's senior national team. Starting in the midfield, Pogba played all 90 minutes in a 3–1 win over Georgia, a country in Eurasia. However, four days later and against a much stronger opponent in Spain, Pogba struggled. In the 76th minute, he was issued a yellow card for a knee to the back of a Spanish player. Then two minutes later, he was shown a second yellow, this time for a late tackle. The two yellow cards resulted in a red card and an ejection from the game. Pogba became the first French national team player to be sent off in only his second match.

For all of Pogba's talent, outbursts such as that have plagued him at times. A few weeks later, on May 5, Juve beat Palermo 1–0 to clinch the Serie A title. But Pogba was again red-carded, this time for spitting at an opponent. He received a three-match suspension.

That summer, France named Pogba as its team captain for the FIFA Under-20 World Cup in Turkey. This was an opportunity to showcase his skills against the best players his age. The group stage was rocky. Once again, Pogba had to miss a match because of yellow cards. But on his return in the quarterfinals, Pogba thrived in his deep midfield position, leading France to two wins and a berth in the final.

In front of more than 20,000 fans, France and Uruguay fought out a defensive battle. With the

Pogba (center) and his France teammates celebrate winning the 2013 FIFA Under-20 World Cup.

score tied 0–0 after 120 minutes, the game went to a shootout. Pogba, not afraid of the pressure, volunteered to shoot first. His goal set the tone as France went on to win 4–1. Pogba, despite scoring only one goal in the tournament, was awarded the golden ball as the most outstanding player.

However, the ups and downs continued in the 2013 Supercoppa Italiana that August. As defending league champions, Juventus played the defending Coppa Italia champion Lazio in the ceremonial game played before each Serie A season. Pogba entered as a 21st-minute sub. Two minutes later, his booming left foot gave Juventus a 1–0 lead. Juve went on to win 4–0. But the celebration was muted because of racist fan behavior. A group of Lazio fans at Stade Olimpico taunted Pogba and fellow black teammates Kwadwo Asamoah and Angelo Ogbonna. Pogba had been warned that this type of behavior might happen in Italy. He vowed to remain focused.

"It's really not nice to come to a football match and hear those sort of things," Pogba said, "but I'm a player, I concentrate on my job."

> **"It's really not nice to come to a football match and hear those sort of things," Pogba said, "but I'm a player, I concentrate on my job."**
>
> **– PAUL POGBA**

When the Serie A season began, Pogba started receiving more regular playing time. By the end of September, he scored his first goal. By the end of November, he had two more. And by the end

Pogba established himself as one of the biggest young stars in the game with Juventus.

of the season, Pogba had scored eight goals and helped Juventus to a third straight Serie A title.

His play was being noticed, too. In December 2013, Italian sports newspaper *Tuttosport* selected him as its European Golden Boy. The paper hands out that honor every year to the best player in Europe younger than 21. A month later, the *Guardian* newspaper in England listed him as one of the 10 most promising players in Europe. Still just 21 years old after that 2013–14 season, Pogba's potential appeared limitless.

Pogba dribbles away from a Ukraine player during their World Cup qualifying playoff.

CHAPTER 6
POGBA AND LES BLEUS

By age 20, Pogba had now played at every level of soccer except one: the World Cup. All signs pointed to that changing in the summer of 2014.

Pogba's road to the World Cup in Brazil got off to a good start. In September 2013, his goal against Belarus helped Les Bleus to a 4–2 win in World Cup qualifying. That marked Pogba's first goal with the senior national team. And he was only getting started.

As Pogba established himself as a regular in France's lineup, however, Les Bleus's qualifying journey hit some bumps. In Europe, the winner of each qualifying group automatically advances to the World Cup. After all 10 games had been played in Group I, France sat in second place, behind Spain. That meant the team would have to take part in a win-or-go-home playoff against another second-place team. So France and Ukraine prepared to face off in a home-and-home series, beginning in Kiev, Ukraine.

Pogba was used to playing as an attacking midfielder at Juventus. But with the national team, the coaches wanted him to take on more defensive responsibilities. Pogba played the full 90 minutes of the match, but in his defensive role he struggled to impact France's attack. Lacking an offensive spark, Les Bleus lost the first leg 2–0.

Missing a World Cup would be unthinkable for France. One of the sport's powers, France had won the tournament in 1998 and reached the final in 2006. But after the 2–0 loss in Kiev, the odds were stacked against Les Bleus. They would have to return to Paris four days later and win by at least three goals, or else they'd be watching the World Cup from home.

This time Pogba's role changed. He was pushed forward more, and he immediately showed how dangerous he could be when he headed a shot over the crossbar in the first 10 minutes. The French kept pressing. Teammate Mamadou Sakho gave Les Bleus the lead in the 22nd minute. Karim Benzema added another goal 12 minutes later. France was now even on aggregate score, but it needed another goal to win the matchup and qualify for the World Cup.

Early in the second half, France got a break. In the 47th minute, Ukraine's Yevhen Khacheridi received his second yellow card. That meant he was ejected. Playing with only 10 men, Ukraine was suddenly the team under pressure. With France continuing to press, Sakho scored the crucial third goal and France won 3–0. With an aggregate score of 3–2 over both games, Les Bleus were on their way to Brazil.

With the qualifying scare behind them, the French arrived in Brazil as contenders. Featuring veteran players such as goalie Hugo Lloris, left back Patrice Evra, and forward Benzema, France boasted one of the world's most talented rosters.

Pogba and teammate Blaise Matuidi lined up as central midfielders in front of a strong back line. Many experts predicted this group would make France a tough team to score against. The big question was whether the team had enough firepower up front. This was especially true with star midfielder Franck Ribery out due to an injury. However, Ribery's absence also presented an opportunity for Pogba to step up.

At only 21 years old, he was the second-youngest player on the team. Only center back Raphael Varane, who was born six weeks after Pogba, was younger. When Pogba scored in a pre-tournament friendly, expectations for a breakout tournament grew.

France opened against Honduras, and Pogba quickly made his presence known. Near the end of the first half, he drew a foul by Wilson Palacios. The foul resulted in a penalty kick, which Benzema converted to put France up 1–0.

Though the play resulted in a goal, it also exposed one of Pogba's weaknesses. He scuffled with the Honduran defender, who picked up his second yellow card and was ejected. But the shoving match could have resulted in Pogba's expulsion, too. So manager Didier Deschamps removed the young star after only 56 minutes as France went on to win 3–0.

After the game, Deschamps publicly criticized Pogba for his attitude. He also removed Pogba from the starting lineup for the next game against Switzerland. When France took a 3–0 lead, Deschamps gave Pogba another chance. The midfielder subbed in at the 63rd minute. Four minutes later, his cross found Benzema for another goal, and France went on to win 5–2.

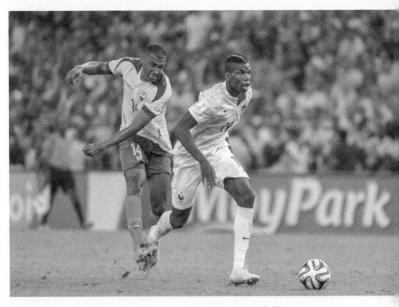

Despite winning their group, Pogba and France failed to inspire during the 2014 World Cup group stage.

With two wins, France needed only one point to secure a spot in the second round. However, the final group stage game didn't instill much confidence among French fans. France and Ecuador played to a 0–0 draw, sending France on. But Pogba struggled. Sportswriters said he was too nervous and committed too many errors. Worst of all, his character was questioned.

Still, Deschamps stuck with his young star and returned him to the starting lineup in the second-round match against Nigeria. Pogba responded with a highly praised performance. In the first half he led a counterattack, sending the ball wide to Mathieu Valbuena. Valbuena then crossed the ball back to the middle of the penalty area, where Pogba met it with a right-footed volley and forced Nigerian goalkeeper Vincent Enyeama into an acrobatic save.

He then positioned himself well on a corner kick in the 79th minute. Enyeama had to come off his line to knock away the corner kick, but the ball deflected across the goal box to Pogba, who alertly jumped and headed it into an open net for a goal. An own-goal by Nigeria's Joseph Yobo in injury time sealed a 2–0 victory, and France advanced to the quarterfinals.

Playing in front of a global audience, Pogba was becoming a sensation in Brazil. With a dash of white through his hair, the player was both flashy and effective. Deschamps even credited the media criticism for improving Pogba's play, forcing the midfielder to concentrate and keep his play simple. The criticism, he said, will "toughen him up."

Meanwhile, Pogba's social media following jumped five-fold to more than three-quarters of a million during the tournament. In the locker room, he won teammates

Eventual champions Germany proved too strong for Pogba and France in the 2014 World Cup quarterfinals.

over with his playful attitude, even leading them in a celebratory cheer as he danced and shouted.

With the spotlight growing, however, the excitement came to an abrupt end in the quarterfinals. A well-organized German team shut down France 1–0. Germany went on to win the tournament, but Pogba went home with some hardware himself. Organizers named him the best young player in the World Cup.

Pogba's star was still rising.

After the World Cup, Pogba returned to Juventus with huge expectations.

CHAPTER 7
STAR OF JUVENTUS

Casual fans who had never heard of Pogba certainly knew his name after the World Cup. He returned to Juventus as one of the brightest young stars in the game. But he also returned to face some new challenges.

Antonio Conte, the manager who had guided Pogba to stardom, left to take over the Italian national team. Massimiliano Allegri replaced him at Juventus. Managerial changes can be dramatic. Each new manager brings new ideas, new playing styles, and new opinions about the players. Pogba had thrived under Conte. Now he'd have to prove himself again under Allegri.

One factor that helped was the arrival of Patrice Evra. The veteran French defender had played with Pogba at Manchester United. "Uncle Pat" had been a father figure to Pogba at Manchester United.

A new contract also helped boost his confidence. After the World Cup, some of Europe's richest teams inquired about Pogba. Fans wondered whether Juventus might sell while his value was high. Instead, in October 2014, the club signed him to a new contract. Pogba's salary rose from €1.5 million (approximately $1.6 million) to €4.5 million ($4.9 million). Only two players in Italy had higher salaries. The deal would also keep Pogba in Torino until 2019.

Keeping Pogba proved to be a smart choice. With his ever-changing hair colors, viral goal celebrations, and fun-loving personality, he was a global star off the field. He was pretty effective on the field, too.

In September, Pogba had set up Carlos Tevez for the winning goal against AC Milan. A month later, he scored the tying goal against Sassuolo and was named man of the match. And less than two weeks after signing his new contract, Pogba scored the winning goal in a Champions League match. Taking a pass from Fernando Llorente at the top of the penalty area,

Pogba scores against Lazio in November 2014.

Pogba tried to backheel the ball to teammate Arturo Vidal streaking past him. But Olympiacos defender Alberto Botia blocked the ball and it bounced back to Pogba. He pirouetted immediately inside the box and hit a low right-footed shot past the goalkeeper. The goal gave Juventus a 3–2 win over the Greek club.

Pogba and Juventus had thrived in the Italian league, having won the previous three Serie A titles (two with Pogba). That domestic success continued under Allegri. But what fans really yearned for was success on the European stage, particularly in the Champions League. Juventus had won the tournament twice, but the last time had been in 1996. Twelve long years had passed since Juve last appeared in the final.

Those hopes took a hit that March. Playing against German club Borussia Dortmund in the round of 16, Pogba lunged to tackle the ball away from a defender. Both players went down. The Dortmund player pulled himself up. Pogba didn't. He clutched his thigh as team medical personnel ran out to help him.

Pogba had to leave the game in the 27th minute. A day later he learned that he had torn a muscle in his thigh and would be out for two months. Thankfully for Pogba, Juventus kept on rolling during his 52-day absence.

By the time Pogba returned in May, Juventus had secured its fourth straight Serie A title. The team had also advanced to the Champions League semifinals, where it beat Spain's Real Madrid 2–1 at home in the first leg. Now, with Pogba back, Juve would have to go on the road, where a draw or win would send the team to the final.

Pogba took his spot in the midfield as more than 78,000 fans at Santiago Bernabeu stadium looked on. No team had won more European championships than Real Madrid. Few stadiums were as intimidating for visitors as Santiago Bernabeu. And few teams had the offensive firepower of Madrid.

All of those advantages paid off in the 23rd minute. Juventus defender Giorgio Chiellini fouled Madrid star James Rodriguez in the penalty box. Cristiano Ronaldo converted the penalty kick, and just like that the series was tied.

On a steamy night in the Spanish capital, Juve continued fighting. That paid off in the 57th minute. On a free kick, Madrid goalie Iker Casillas punched the ball away, but the ball went to Pogba off to the side of the goal. He headed the ball back across the box to teammate Alvaro Morata, who stopped it with his chest and blasted it into the back of the net. Once again, Juventus was ahead.

The Madrid players desperately tried to come back, but every attempt was snuffed out. Pogba nearly sealed it in the 88th minute. Instead, Casillas got his hand on

Pogba shields the ball from Real Madrid's Isco during their Champions League game at Santiago Bernabeu.

his shot. Still, after two more minutes in regulation and four minutes of injury time, Juventus held on. With a 3–2 score over the two games, the Italian team was on to the Champions League final in June.

That left time for Juve to take care of some other business. In May, the team defeated Lazio 3–2 to claim its first Coppa Italia championship in 20 years. However, the high from that event was toned down 10 days later. Juventus ended the Serie A season with a 2–2 draw against Verona. After the game, Allegri scolded Pogba for "too much showboating." Pogba responded that it was his personality, not arrogance. Still, he took Allegri's scolding as advice.

The Champions League final was held on June 6 at Olympiastadion in Berlin, Germany. After outlasting one Spanish giant in the semifinals, Juventus was now faced with another one. And this test would be even harder. Barcelona had been one of the strongest teams in Europe for years. Featuring offensive stars such as Lionel Messi, Luis Suarez, and Neymar, the team knew how to control possession and score in bunches. Any mistakes would be punished.

Unfortunately for Juventus, those mistakes came early and often. Ivan Rakitic put Barcelona up in the fourth minute. Seven minutes later, Juventus's Vidal was issued a yellow card. Pogba received one himself in the 41st. Still, Juve was not out of it. Just after halftime, in the 55th minute, Morata tied the game. However, Suarez restored Barcelona's lead in the 68th minute, and Neymar finished it off in injury time for a 3–1 Juventus loss.

The result was disappointing, but the future was still bright for Pogba. He had scored 10 goals in 41 games in all competitions during the 2014–15 season. At 22 years old, he was one of Europe's most sought-after players. And in July, he was named one of 10 finalists for UEFA's Best Player in Europe Award.

The momentum only continued in 2015–16. Going into that season, Allegri gave Pogba new responsibilities in the midfield. In his new role, Pogba would have more time on the ball and room for creativity. He would also have the No. 10 jersey. That is a huge honor on most teams, and Pogba would join a list of Juventus No. 10s that included legends such as Roberto Baggio, Michel Platini, and Alessandro Del Piero.

With his role on the team growing, Pogba stepped up. Though Juventus again fell short of Champions League, losing in the round of 16, the club won its fifth

Pogba (left) and teammate Andrea Pirlo (right) try to stop Barcelona's Lionel Messi in the 2015 Champions League final.

straight Serie A title while also defending its Coppa Italia win. Pogba, meanwhile, played in a team-high 49 games, again scoring 10 goals. All the while, more organizations and publications were recognizing him as one of the best players in the world. And all of Europe's biggest clubs wanted him.

With a special new hairstyle, Pogba set out for a
European championship on home soil.

CHAPTER 8
ALL IN ON EUROPE

Pogba had moved away from France as a teenager. In the summer of 2016, he had an opportunity to come home and do something special. That year's European Championship, known as Euro 2016, was held in France. And with Pogba in the midfield, the home team was one of the favorites.

For the occasion, Pogba arrived with a Gallic rooster shaved into the side of his head, mimicking the French team's crest. He and his teammates were ready to make a statement on the field, too. But early in the tournament, the statement seemed to be that they were rusty.

As the hosts, France didn't have to qualify for Euro 2016. The lack of competitive games showed in the opener against Romania. With a 1–1 draw looming, Pogba was subbed out. Only an 89th-minute goal saved the heavily favored French team from embarrassment. And afterward, Pogba took much of the blame. Commentators said he lacked "precision" and "coherence." For someone considered to be among the best in the world, this was not what was expected.

Five days later against another underdog in Albania, both Pogba and forward Antoine Griezmann began on the substitute's bench. France manager Didier Deschamps was sending a message to his two young stars. Without them, however, France again played below expectations. Pogba entered to start the second half, and Griezmann followed in the 68th minute. But as the game neared the 90th minute, the score remained 0–0. Only then did Griezmann score to save France, and then Dimitri Payet added another for a 2–0 victory.

Pogba raced over to congratulate Payet for his goal. However, he also made a rude gesture to the press. It was little surprise, then, that the press corps shot back. In addition to calling out Pogba's gesture, the press singled him out for poor passing, losing the ball too easily, and his generally blundering play.

One person not swayed by the press was Deschamps. He restored Pogba to the starting lineup for the final group game against Switzerland. If France won or drew, it would win the group and face a weaker team in the second round. However, a Swiss win would give them the group win.

Shifted to the left side of the midfield, Pogba's play improved. The result, though, remained uninspiring. France did only as much as it had to and tied Switzerland 0–0. Still, Les Bleus had done well enough to finish atop Group A and earn a second-round match against Ireland.

If Pogba's play looked like it was improving against Switzerland, he committed a huge mistake against Ireland. His leg clipped the heels of Shane Long in the penalty area, and Ireland was awarded a penalty kick. Robbie Brady converted, and Ireland was ahead 1–0 only two minutes after the opening kickoff.

The score stayed that way until Griezmann rescued France with a pair of goals early in the second half. After a rocky start, Griezmann's standout performance propelled France to a 2–1 victory.

The win put France against a surprising Iceland team in the quarterfinals, and this time France rolled

Pogba rises high into the air to score on a header against Iceland.

a 5–2 win. Pogba scored with a header from a corner kick to give France a 2–0 lead. It was his first goal for Les Bleus in a year and a half. Finally, it appeared, Pogba and his teammates were finding their form.

That continued in the semifinals against Germany, the defending World Cup champs. Griezmann converted a penalty in the first half. In the 72nd minute, Pogba set up Griezmann for another goal. France won 2–0 and was on to the final.

The French players were feeling good. Their opponent, Portugal, had made a surprise run to the final. Despite featuring a superstar in forward Cristiano Ronaldo, the team had gotten some lucky breaks. It advanced through the group stage without winning a game and then enjoyed a relatively easy path to the final. With the game at home in Paris's iconic Stade de France, the French players were feeling confident. That confidence only grew in the 25th minute, when Ronaldo was carried off the field with a knee injury. With Portugal now missing its best player, the French had even more reason to believe they were on their way to their first major championship since winning Euro 2000. Unfortunately, as Pogba revealed later, they might have been too confident.

"When we beat Germany, we thought it was the final," he said. "We thought we'd won the final before playing it, which was a mistake."

After 90 minutes, the game was still tied 0–0. In extra time, though, Portugal forward Eder hit a blast from 25 yards. France couldn't match it in the final 10 minutes, and Les Bleus were done. Pogba lay flat on his back. Now the French had to watch as Portugal celebrated the European title on their home field.

The tournament was a massive blow to Pogba and his teammates. The press criticized him as an "intermittent performer" with an indifferent attitude. Even members of the Italian media said they had seen only a "ghost" of Pogba and criticized him for missing opportunities. It was an evaluation that was in sharp contrast to his career up to that point. But it wouldn't affect his future prospects.

Pogba and his teammates could hardly believe it when they lost to Portugal in the Euro 2016 final.

Fans around the world were eager to find out where Pogba would end up playing club soccer in the 2016–17 season.

CHAPTER 9
THE WORLD'S MOST EXPENSIVE MAN

The European Championship did little to dampen the speculation about Pogba's future. After helping establishing Juventus as Italy's premier team, the player appeared ready for a new challenge.

Fans and sportswriters alike wondered where he might play in 2016–17. Would he move to Real Madrid, where his childhood idol Zinedine Zidane had just been named manager? Would he move to Paris-St. Germain, the club he grew up watching? What about Manchester United, the team he left in tears four years earlier? Seemingly every big club in Europe was in consideration.

Following Euro 2016, Pogba went to the United States for a much-needed vacation. But he didn't take a break from feeding the rumors. He posted daily on Instagram and Twitter: pictures from Los Angeles of himself with Romelu Lukaku, the Belgian striker who at the time was under contract to Chelsea. Los Angeles chef Bobby Chinn posted selfies with Pogba and Swedish striker Zlatan Ibrahimovic, sparking rumors that Pogba was going to Manchester United, where Ibrahimovic had just moved.

Pogba flew with Lukaku on a private jet to Florida for more vacation and more selfies. Then to Las Vegas. Then to New York City. News reports followed his posts and tried to interpret each one. A black-and-white picture of him on the famous US Route 66 showed Pogba in red-tinted shoes and a red baseball cap. Some were sure this meant he was returning to the Red Devils of Manchester United.

Pogba posted another picture of him giving Canadian rapper Drake his No. 10 Juventus jersey. Surely, many wrote, this was a sign that he was giving up on Juventus. And still another selfie showed up, this one posted by a fan on vacation. He ran into Pogba in Los Angeles and had him sign his Man U jersey.

The three weeks of rumors, guesses, and theories finally came to an end shortly after midnight on August 9, 2016—but not without drama.

Manchester United posted a nine-second video titled, "Are you ready? Pogback." It depicted a man with his face hidden by shadows looking very much like Pogba in a Manchester United sweatshirt with the hood up.

Then approximately an hour later, the official word came. Manchester United issued a formal press release announcing Pogba's transfer. More videos followed, including one by Manchester United in which Pogba stepped out of the shadow to say: "I'm back." Adidas put out its own video of Pogba dancing with rapper Stormzy.

The news sent shock waves through the soccer community. Then Juventus shook things up further. The Italian club announced it had sold Pogba's contract for €105 million ($116 million). That surpassed the record €100 million Real Madrid paid for Gareth Bale three years earlier (exchange rates at the time meant Bale's transfer equaled $132 million).

As part of the move, Pogba signed a five-year contract with his former team. His salary would jump

Pogba joined Zlatan Ibrahimovic (right) and other huge stars at Manchester United.

three-fold, to €14 million ($16 million) a year. Plus, he'd receive another €5 million ($5.8 million) for his image rights.

This all begged the question: was Pogba crazy?

After all, he had left Manchester United only four years earlier because manager Alex Ferguson wouldn't play him. Then he thrived playing in Italy, where the team gave him an opportunity and room for creativity in the midfield. So why would he go back?

One reason was that Ferguson had since retired. Jose Mourinho, another accomplished manager, was now in charge. Pogba also had some unfinished business there.

"I feel the time is right to go back to Old Trafford," he said, referring to the club's famous stadium. "I always enjoyed playing in front of the fans and can't wait to make my contribution to the team. This is the right club for me to achieve everything I hope to in the game."

> "I feel the time is right to go back to Old Trafford. I always enjoyed playing in front of the fans and can't wait to make my contribution to the team."
>
> **– PAUL POGBA**

Manchester United had struggled in the years since Ferguson retired. But with Mourinho at the helm and Pogba in the midfield, expectations grew for 2016–17.

"He is quick, strong, scores goals, and reads the game better than many players much older than he is," Mourinho said. "At 23, he has the chance to make that position his own here over many years. He is young and will continue to improve; he has the chance to be at the heart of this club for the next decade and beyond."

The record transfer fee, and comments such as those, put added pressure on Pogba when he didn't immediately live up to the expectations.

In September, United lost at home to Manchester City. Afterward, former player-turned-analyst Jamie Carragher blasted Pogba for being out of position often, saying he was "like a kid in the school yard." This was the new reality for the world's most expensive player.

Pogba had moments of success, including scoring his first league goal that September and adding two more in a Europa League match one month later. But even when he played well, criticism was a near constant.

In his first season back, Pogba was the team's fifth-leading scorer with nine goals in 49 games across

Pogba and Henrikh Mkhitaryan celebrate a
Manchester United goal in the 2017 Europa League
final against Ajax.

all competitions. Manchester United won the Europa League and the English League Cup. Pogba even scored in the Europa League final, a 2–0 win over Dutch club Ajax. It was Manchester United's first European title in nine years. However, he also had the second-most yellow cards (10) on the team, and United finished sixth in the English Premier League standings. Plus, fans cared more about the Champions League and FA Cup than the Europa League and League Cup. In short, they expected much better.

There was also personal tragedy in Pogba's first season. On May 12, his father died at the age of 79. When Pogba returned to Manchester United after the funeral, he scored in the team's final game of the season, a 2–0 win over Crystal Palace. He pointed to the sky in a tribute to his dad.

Although fans were kind to Pogba on this day, their reviews of his first season were not. One called him a "disappointment," not the "game-dominating monster" people were expecting. Others pointed to Pogba's social media, where the soccer star was showing off his latest haircuts or fashionable outfits. One report, in the *Daily Mirror* tabloid newspaper, claimed the team had told him to "rein in his social media activity and concentrate on delivering the high-level performances they know he is capable of."

Through good times and bad, Pogba has made time to support others. He has donated money to organizations such as the International Red Cross and leaned on his popular social media accounts to raise money and support for other causes. In 2017, he also launched his own charity. Along with brothers Florentin and Mathias—both of whom became pro soccer players as well—he created the Pogba Foundation. The goal, he said, is "to make the world better and inspire others to do the same."

For Manchester United fans, though, they simply wanted to see Pogba live up to their expectations on the pitch. His second season started out well. He scored in the season opener, a 4–0 win against West Ham. But less than a month later he tore his hamstring during a Champions League game and missed eight weeks. By the end of the year, Pogba had scored even fewer goals than in his first season: six in 33 games. He had fewer yellow cards (six), but he was also ejected with a red card in one game.

Meanwhile, the team struggled at times, too. Manchester United didn't last past the round of 16 in the Champions League or the fifth round in the League Cup. Though the team made a run to the FA Cup final, it lost there to Chelsea.

What had gone wrong? Some pundits blamed Pogba, who turned 25 that March. They said he was undisciplined and lackluster on defense. At one point, Mourinho played 21-year-old English midfielder Scott McTominay in Pogba's place for several games. Other observers, however, blamed Mourinho. They saw Pogba as a dynamic talent who was limited in Mourinho's rigid system. This invariably led to rumors that Pogba might be ready to switch teams again. One report even had him going to the other local team, Manchester City.

The good news for Manchester United was that it ended up finishing second in the Premier League, the team's best finish in five years. And the good news for Pogba was that he had an opportunity to show he was still the player many thought he would be. Soon after the season ended, Pogba was back with his France teammates preparing for the 2018 World Cup.

Pogba's first two seasons at Manchester United left fans wondering what had happened to the superstar they saw at Juventus.

The big question going into the 2018 World Cup was whether Pogba and his French teammates could put the team before their individual stardom.

CHAPTER 10
THE WORLD AS A STAGE

There was no doubting France's talent. Perhaps no team entered the 2018 World Cup in Russia with more individual talent on the roster. The question was whether Les Bleus could put it all together as a team and win the World Cup. To answer that question, many focused on Pogba.

Soccer fans had seen his talent, his versatility, and his ability to control a game. But they had seen his shortcomings, too, especially during the past two seasons. Once thought of as France's key player for a generation, Pogba now entered the World Cup with questions of whether he was overrated. He had the ability, but did he have the focus and desire to lead France all the way?

Pogba's goal secured a 2–1 win over Australia, but France failed to dominate against the weaker opponent.

Manager Didier Deschamps had a plan. As a tough-minded defensive midfielder, he had captained France to its first World Cup title in 1998. He brought a no-nonsense approach to his new role, too. Deschamps saw that, as in 1998, several French players were the stars for their club teams, used to being the focal point of the attack and scoring a lot of goals. For France, he wanted those players to accept less-glamorous roles with an emphasis on defending. The player being asked the most, perhaps, was Pogba.

Pogba was used to playing with freedom and offensive creativity. At his best, he was able to break free from his role and lead a devastating attack. For France, Deschamps asked him to play as a deep central midfielder, lining up to the left of N'Golo Kante. His job would be to slow the world's best midfielders while supporting France's other talented attackers. For a player used to the spotlight, this would be a big change. He accepted the challenge.

"It is a World Cup and we have to sacrifice," Pogba said. "We have to defend. It's not what I do best, but I do it with pleasure. We have the same objective, and it is to win. I think I have become more mature and all the other players help me a lot on that."

Pundits questioned whether Pogba could do it. Would the 25-year-old accept his less flashy role, or would he become bored and try to take over a game by himself? Pogba provided a hint of what was to come upon his arrival in Russia. Unlike in previous high-profile games, Pogba arrived with a simple haircut: shaved short, and with no added color.

"It is a World Cup and we have to sacrifice."

– PAUL POGBA

The group stage showed France's potential, but it also highlighted some of its challenges. In the opener, Les Bleus overcame Australia 2–1, with Pogba playing an instrumental role in both goals. But the overall performance against a weaker opponent felt uninspired.

Pogba was also influential in France's 1–0 victory over Peru, a win that assured Les Bleus would advance to the second round. That took the drama out of the third game. With Pogba carrying a yellow card, Deschamps left the midfielder on the bench for a 0–0 draw against Denmark. Just like that, France had won its group and moved on. But with those score lines, few fans were thrilled by the team's performance.

"When I dance and score, I hear nobody. When I dance, and we lose, then it is a problem. It is fine, though, I will continue, despite the critics. You say I am a showman, but I am just me—take me as I am."

— PAUL POGBA

Although Les Bleus had yet to win fans over with their play on the field, Pogba made headlines off of it before the Denmark game. In his first press conference with the national team in four years, he pushed back against his critics.

"I do not really understand—you only talk of the negative," he said. "When I dance and score, I hear nobody. When I dance, and we lose, then it is a problem. It is fine, though, I will continue, despite the critics. You say I am a showman, but I am just me—take me as I am."

France had a wake-up call in the round of 16. Awaiting Les Bleus was a desperate Argentina team. France had allowed only one goal in the group stage, but Argentina boasted attacking talent unlike France's first three opponents. Leading the way was Lionel Messi. One of the best players of all time, Messi had one thing missing from his resume: a World Cup title. Pogba and Kante would need to play a big role if France were to stop him.

Argentina started well, controlling the possession and creating early opportunities. But France took the lead when Kylian Mbappe drew a penalty and Antoine Griezmann converted. However, the South Americans recovered and tied the game just before halftime when Angel Di Maria was left unmarked 30 yards from goal. With Pogba out on the wing guarding another player, Di Maria unleashed a left-footed drive that curled past French goalkeeper Hugo Lloris.

Pogba and teammate Olivier Giroud celebrate France's wild win over Argentina.

Things were still looking good for France, but that changed three minutes into the second half. Messi settled a blocked shot in the French penalty area, dribbled around, and then blasted a shot past Pogba and midfielder Blaise Matuidi. Argentina's Gabriel Mercado, left alone in front of the net, deflected the ball into the goal.

Just like that, France was down 2–1. Not only were Les Bleus trailing for the first time, they were trailing against one of the world's best players. That seemed to wake up France. Nine minutes later, Benjamin Pavard equalized for France with a long-range strike. Then Mbappe added two goals of his own as France averted disaster, eventually winning 4–3.

The win was a relief for France. The feeling on the other sideline was one of despair. After celebrating the victory, Pogba noticed a clearly distraught Messi. He walked up from behind and put his right arm around him. Messi acknowledged the gesture by tapping Pogba's arm. Some took it as a sign of Pogba's maturity.

Pogba and France had little time to celebrate, though. Up next was another dangerous South American team in Uruguay. Behind strikers Luis Suarez and Edinson Cavani, Uruguay was a pesky opponent that some experts thought could make a run. But those plans were dashed when Uruguay met France. With Pogba and Kante clogging up the center of the field, Uruguay's attack was declawed. France won 2–0 to move on to the semifinals.

After their slow start, Les Bleus were now a clear favorite. Observers who wondered about Pogba's patience and discipline were beginning to talk of those qualities as strengths. Pogba's effective play from one box to the other was stifling opposing midfields and giving France's attackers the freedom to create plays.

France's biggest test, though, was still to come. The way the bracket worked out, many of the favored teams were on one side. So when France and Belgium met in the semifinals, it was a meeting of the tournament's two remaining favorites.

In a tournament with no shortage of offense, Belgium had proven to be the most lethal. Once again, though, France shut down Belgium's stars with its pragmatic style. The Belgians struggled to move the ball beyond the middle of the field, where Pogba and Kante continued to dominate. One goal from Samuel Umtiti was enough to send France on to the final with a 1–0 win.

In a tournament filled with surprise results, France reaching the final was one of the few things to go as planned. But many expected France to make it there by playing a more exciting style of soccer.

France's opponent, meanwhile, was a team few expected to see there. Croatia had never played in a World Cup final before. Behind a golden generation of players, the team proved to be one of the most effective sides in the tournament. The Croatians had cruised through one of the World Cup's most difficult groups, winning all three games by a combined score of 7–1. Then they survived the knockout round, including winning two games in a shootout. Their semifinal went to extra time, too, meaning they played the equivalent of an entire extra game. But behind star players Ivan Perisic, Luka Modric, and Ivan Rakitic, Croatia had shown the ability to play with anyone.

This proved to be a concern for France fans. Just as in Euro 2016, France had the more talented team. That meant the pressure was on Les Bleus to live up to their ability. Yet going into the game, the French players brushed off the notion that they were under any pressure. Before the final, Pogba gathered his teammates together.

Pogba passes against Croatia's Ivan Rakitic during the 2018 World Cup final.

"I want this evening to be in the memory of all the French people who are watching us," he told them. "Their children, their children's children, and their children's children's children. Today, there are 90 minutes to get back into history for life."

The game kicked off at Luzhniki Stadium in Moscow, Russia. All eyes were on how Pogba and France would slow Modric and Croatia's other attackers. Early on, Croatia controlled the possession. France needed to settle it down.

That happened in the 18th minute. Presented a free kick, Griezmann sent the ball into the box. Pogba, using his height, worked at the edge of the goal box. His presence there helped create enough confusion that defender Mario Mandzukic strained to get the top of his head to the ball. It was just enough to deflect it past his own goalkeeper.

Rather than be frazzled by the mistake, Croatia fought on. That paid off 10 minutes later when Perisic scored to tie the game 1–1. But France took the lead again immediately before halftime when Griezmann scored on a penalty kick.

Throughout the tournament, Pogba had played the disciplined, team-first role Deschamps had planned. That allowed teammates such as Mbappe and Griezmann to take starring roles offensively. Now, finally, it was Pogba's time to really shine offensively.

Fourteen minutes into the second half, France worked a counterattack down the right side. Mbappe played a short ball into the middle of the penalty area to Griezmann. With a Croatian defender on his back, Griezmann played the ball back to Pogba, who was trailing the play at the edge of the arc.

Pogba volleyed the ball with a thunderous right-footed shot. But it struck Modric in the middle of the penalty area and slowly bounced back toward Pogba. This time he used his left foot from the 18 and hit another thunderous drive. The ball sailed into the left side of the net while Croatian goalkeeper Danijel Subasic simply fell backward, unable to react.

It was another Pogboom and a moment of redemption for Pogba. For all the criticism, for all of the people who said he was overrated, Pogba had just given France a 3–1 lead with only 30 minutes to go in the World Cup final. It became a virtually insurmountable lead six minutes later when Mbappe added a long-range strike of his own. And when Mandzukic scored for Croatia to make it 4–2, that meant Pogba's goal proved to be the game winner.

With a heavy rain pouring onto the field, Pogba ran and slid across the grass in celebration. "It's just unbelievable, magnificent, wonderful, a dream come true," Pogba said. As for the critics who doubted him and his teammates? "We invite them to celebrate with us," he said.

Known for his flamboyance, Pogba had been more reserved during the World Cup. In the aftermath, he

With their win over Croatia, Pogba and France were champions of the world.

let his personality come out once again. After the final, Pogba led his teammates in crashing Deschamps's press conference, soaking their stern manager with a beverage. Pogba danced on the table. He even led French President Emmanuel Macron in his famous "dab" celebration.

For Pogba, it was a moment to savor. Once again he had shown that he was one of the best players in the world—and this time, he did so playing a style that many doubted he could.

TIMELINE

1993

Paul Labile Pogba is born on March 15 in Roissy-en-Brie, France.

1999

Pogba joins the US Roissy soccer team. In 2006, he moves to the bigger US Torcy soccer club. One year later he moves to Le Havre AC.

2009

On July 30, Pogba signs with Manchester United in England.

2011

Pogba makes his first-team debut with Manchester United on September 20, a 3–0 victory over Leeds United in the League Cup.

2012

On July 3, Pogba announces he's transferring to Juventus in Italy.

2013

Pogba is named best player of the FIFA Under-20 World Cup as he leads France to victory.

2014

Pogba is named the best young player of the World Cup as France makes a run to the quarterfinals.

2016

Pogba leads France to the final of the European Championship on home soil, but Les Bleus fall to Portugal.

2016

On August 9, Manchester United pays a record €105 million ($116 million) to bring Pogba back.

2018

Playing a more defensive role, Pogba helps lead France to the World Cup title, defeating Croatia in the final.

FACT SHEET

- **Name:** Paul Labile Pogba
- **Born:** March 15, 1993, in Lagny-sur-Marne, France
- **Height:** 6-foot-3
- **Weight:** 185 pounds
- **Position:** attacking midfielder
- **Amateur/developmental teams:** US Roissy, US Torcy, Le Havre AC
- **Professional teams:** Manchester United (2011–2012, 2016–); Juventus (2012–2016)

BY THE NUMBERS

World Cup 2014
- **Games Played:** 5
- **Minutes Played:** 354
- **Goals:** 1

World Cup 2018
- **Games Played:** 6
- **Minutes Played:** 539
- **Goals:** 1

Record Transfer Fee
- **Juventus to Manchester United:** €105 million ($116 million)

CAREER AWARDS

- 2018 FIFA World Cup champion
- 2017 Europa Cup champion
- 2013, 2014, 2015, 2016 Serie A champion
- 2015, 2016 Coppa Italia champion
- 2015 FIFPro World XI
- 2014 FIFA World Cup Best Young Player
- 2013 FIFA Under-20 World Cup champion
- 2013 FIFA Under-20 World Cup Golden Ball

FAMILY

- **Father:** Antoine Fassou Pogba
- **Mother:** Yeo Moriba
- **Brothers:** Florentin and Mathias
- **Florentin Peile Pogba:** Born August 19, 1990. Developed in the Celta de Vigo youth system in Spain. Made professional debut with Sedan in 2011 before transferring to Saint-Etienne in France and later Genclerbirligi in Turkey.
- **Mathias Fassou Pogba:** Born August 19, 1990. Developed in Celta de Vigo youth system. Made professional debut with French fourth-division club Quimper before going on to play with Wrexham, Crewe Alexandra, and Crawley Town in England; Pescara in Italy; Partick Thistle in Scotland; and Sparta Rotterdam in the Netherlands. Both Florentin and Mathias have played for the Guinean national team.

FOR MORE INFORMATION

BOOKS

Bader, Bonnie. *What Is the World Cup?* New York: Penguin Workshop, 2018.

Karpovich, Todd. *Manchester United*. Minneapolis: Abdo Publishing, 2017.

McDougall, Chrös. *The Best Soccer Players of All Time*. Minneapolis: Abdo Publishing, 2015.

WEBSITES

FIFA World Cup
www.fifa.com/worldcup

France Football
www.francefootball.fr

Paul Pogba Player Page
www.manutd.com/en/players-and-staff/detail/paul-pogba

PLACES TO VISIT

OLD TRAFFORD

Sir Matt Busby Way
Stretford, Manchester M16 0RA, UK
+44 161 868 8000
www.manutd.com/en/visit-old-trafford

Seating more than 70,000 fans, Old Trafford has been Manchester United's home stadium since 1910. The iconic stadium is sometimes called "The Theater of Dreams."

STADE DE FRANCE

93200 Saint-Denis, France
+33 1 55 93 00 00
www.stadefrance.com/en

Home of the French national team, Stade de France is located in the Paris suburb of Saint-Denis and seats more than 80,000 fans. The French national team won the 1998 World Cup here, though it was also the site of the losing effort in the Euro 2016 final.

SELECT BIBLIOGRAPHY

"Guinea (The World Factbook)." *Central Intelligence Agency*, www.cia.gov/library/publications/the-world-factbook/geos/gv.html. Accessed 4 Oct. 2018.

Johnston, Neil. "Real Madrid 1–1 Juventus." *BBC Sport*, 13 May 2015, www.bbc.com/sport/football/32683303.

Masters, James. "Paul Pogba Signs for Manchester United." *CNN*, 8 Aug. 2018, http://cnn.it/2aHGuE2.

McNulty, Phil. "Juventus 1–3 Barcelona." *BBC Sport*, 6 June 2015, www.bbc.com/sport/football/33010277.

Nicholson, Tom. "Watch Paul Pogba Give France a World Cup Final Pep Talk." Esquire, 20 July 2018, www.esquire.com/uk/latest-news/a22495462/watch-paul-pogba-give-frances-world-cup-final-pep-talk/.

"Paul Pogba." *FIFA.com*, www.fifa.com/worldcup/players/player/367388/. Accessed 4 Oct. 2018.

"Paul Pogba Joins Manchester United." *Juventus*, 9 Aug. 2016, www.juventus.com/en/news/news/2016/paul-pogba-joins-manchester-united.php.

"Paul Pogba Strikes for France in Victory over Netherlands."
Sky Sports, 11 Oct. 2016, www.skysports.com/football/
netherlands-vs-france/350055.

Press Association. "Manchester United Reach Agreement over
Pogba." *The Independent*, 18 June 2010, www.independent.
co.uk/sport/football/premier-league/manchester-united-reach-
agreement-over-pogba-2004018.html.

Rej, Arindam. "Manchester United's Paul Pogba Used to Cry after
Defeats—Former Coach." *ESPN*, 6 Jan. 2017, www.espn.co.uk/
football/manchester-united/story/3032990/manchester-uniteds-
paul-pogba-used-to-cry-after-defeats-former-coach.

Voakes, Kris. "How Pogba Finally Became a Man at World Cup
Following Manchester United Struggles." *Goal*, http://shr.gs/
cekgYwF. Accessed 4 Oct. 2018.

Wallace, Sam. "Paul Pogba: The Inside Story of the World's Most
Expensive Footballer." *The Telegraph*, 11 Aug. 2016, www.
telegraph.co.uk/football/2016/08/11/paul-pogba-the-inside-
story-of-the-worlds-most-expensive-footbal/.

INDEX

ABOUT THE AUTHOR

Brian Trusdell has been a sportswriter for more than 30 years, with work including writing for the Associated Press and Bloomberg News. He has reported from six Olympics and four World Cups, and he has traveled to every continent except Antarctica. Trusdell lives in New Jersey with his wife and daughter.